Superhero's Magick

S ROB

DEDICATION

I dedicate this book to my mother and father.

CONTENTS

ACKNOWLEDGMENTS

I acknowledge the existence of real magick.

Chapter 1 Protection

In this world there exists magick, real magick the one thing no one told you about or worse led you to believe that it didn't exist, that it was a lie, a myth, something of legend only and so out of reach, something you could not have even if you were special and not the humdrum person you were led to believe you were. I will not lie to you; you are not humdrum you are special and capable of special things. However, the true power of your gifts comes not in always what they are but in what you choose to do with them, how you choose to affect the world with them. The fact is that the true superhero uses his or her abilities to change the world to fight the forces which harm others, sometimes on a mass scale. But in truth it is just as important to inspire others because if you are a good example people will try and take some of that spirit you represent into their own lives and so the effect is magnified and there is more goodness in the world. But first you must be able to protect yourself and so I will be showing you how to draw upon the power of voodoo to gain protection.

For the protective magick that follows you will be using Papa Legba he also known as the Voodoo Man himself and is believed by many to be Saint Peter and he controls a doorway and through this doorway we shall summon through Ti-Jean-Petro an occultist and a dwarf with one leg. In fact, we shall then be asking Ti-Jean-Petro for what we desire; in our case here protection. This magick works therefore like this, Papa Legba opens the doorway, we summon Ti-Jean-Petro we ask Ti-Jean-Petro for what we want, Ti-Jean Petro leaves back through the doorway and we get Papa Legba to shut the doorway closed. But you shall need to do all of this while wishing real magick to be worked; but if you do this then it will. Protective magick is good to practice because we always need it and it is great to use when we cannot think of anything else, we need. The magick for protection follows.

Superhero protective magick

Papa Legba the Voodoo Man himself, he known as Saint Peter, the old man with walking cane and with stick in hand you walk with a limp but only because you have one foot always in one world and the other foot in another because you control the doorway that swings many ways and to many places. Papa Legba open the doorway, open the doorway here and now: Papa Legba does open the doorway, the doorway opens it is open here and now. I call Ti-Jean-Petro the one-legged dwarf, the powerful mage through the doorway. Ti-Jean-Petro come through the doorway and be here with me: Ti-Jean-Petro does come through the doorway and is here with me. Ti-Jean-Petro I ask that you help me, protect me from all disease, all attacks no matter who or what is the attacker no matter what means they utilize and this is what I ask of you. Ti-Jean-Petro agrees to help and departs back through the doorway. Papa Legba the Voodoo Man himself, he known as Saint Peter, the old man with walking cane and with stick in hand you walk with a limp but only because you have one foot always in one world and the other foot in another because you control the doorway that swings many ways and to many places. Papa Legba shut the doorway, shut the doorway here and now: Papa Legba does shut the doorway, the doorway closes it is shut here and now. So it is and will be.

As a would-be superhero you need not just to protect yourself but also your home because this would otherwise be a terrible vulnerability and we should not forget that there are times when being a superhero makes us not popular but unloved even. The truth is that most people feel happier when things are grey rather than when they are all true and moral. You must protect yourself if you wish to help others and so here is more protective magick which I believe you should use; and here it is.

4

Superhero magick to protect your home

(You should be at home to work this magick)

Papa Legba the Voodoo Man himself, he known as Saint Peter, the old man with walking cane and with stick in hand you walk with a limp but only because you have one foot always in one world and the other foot in another because you control the doorway that swings many ways and to many places. Papa Legba open the doorway, open the doorway here and now: Papa Legba does open the doorway, the doorway opens it is open here and now. I call Ti-Jean-Petro the one-legged dwarf, the powerful mage through the doorway. Ti-Jean-Petro come through the doorway and be here with me: Ti-Jean-Petro does come through the doorway and is here with me. Ti-Jean-Petro I ask that you help me by protecting where I live protect my home that I am in right now and this is what I ask of you. Ti-Jean-Petro agrees to help and departs back through the doorway. Papa Legba the Voodoo Man himself, he known as Saint

Peter, the old man with walking cane and with stick in hand you walk with a limp but only because you have one foot always in one world and the other foot in another because you control the doorway that swings many ways and to many places. Papa Legba shut the doorway, shut the doorway here and now: Papa Legba does shut the doorway, the doorway closes it is shut here and now. So it is and will be.

We all need protection for those we love and so I have included this magick for family: I know your loved ones and your family aren't always the same people. However, when our families are in trouble quite often, we are too. I feel that since magick is essentially free: although the book isn't: you get endless spell casts for free because you are learning how to do them yourself. Here's magick to protect your family.

Superhero magick to protect your family

Papa Legba the Voodoo Man himself, he known as Saint Peter, the old man with walking cane and with stick in hand you walk with a limp but only because you have one foot always in one world and the other foot in another because you control the doorway that swings many ways and to many places. Papa Legba open the doorway, open the doorway here and now: Papa Legba does open the doorway, the doorway opens it is open here and now. I call Ti-Jean-Petro the one-legged dwarf, the powerful mage through the doorway. Ti-Jean-Petro come through the doorway and be here with me: Ti-Jean-Petro does come through the doorway and is here with me. Ti-Jean-Petro I ask that you protect my family protect them from all harm and this is what I ask of you. Ti-Jean-Petro agrees to help and departs back through the doorway. Papa Legba the Voodoo Man himself, he known as Saint Peter, the old man with walking cane and with stick in hand you walk with a limp but only because you have one foot always in one world and the other foot in another because you control the doorway that swings many ways and to many places. Papa Legba shut the doorway, shut the doorway here and now: Papa Legba does shut the doorway, the doorway closes it is shut here and now. So it is and will be.

This following magick is so you can protect anyone you desire and so could be considered to be the first magick to help others you are not related to in some way: this magick can work on anyone although it is easier if you know their name and what they look like. Will this magick to work and it shall.

Superhero magick to protect a chosen person

Papa Legba the Voodoo Man himself, he known as Saint Peter, the old man with walking cane and with stick in hand you walk with a limp but only because you have one foot always in one world and the other foot in another because you control the doorway that swings many ways and to many places. Papa Legba open the doorway, open the doorway here and now: Papa Legba does open the doorway, the doorway opens it is open here and now. I call Ti-Jean-Petro the one-legged dwarf, the powerful mage through the doorway. Ti-Jean-Petro come through the doorway and be here with me: Ti-Jean-Petro does come through the doorway and is here with me. Ti-Jean-Petro I ask that you protect <u>state name of chosen person</u> from all disease, all attacks no matter who or what is the attacker no matter what means they utilize and this is what I ask of you. Ti-Jean-Petro agrees to help and departs back through the doorway. Papa Legba the Voodoo Man himself, he known as Saint Peter, the old man with walking cane and with stick in hand you walk with a limp but only because you have one foot always in one world and the other foot in another because you control the doorway that swings many ways and to many places. Papa Legba shut the doorway, shut the doorway here and now: Papa Legba does shut the doorway, the doorway closes it is shut here and now. So it is and will be.

You now have enough protective magick to have made the first step to superherodom. I know that in reality we need to help others to gain the moniker superhero, but you shall gain what you need as you proceed through the book. Yes, my would-be superhero your powers are growing.

Chapter 2 Freeing slaves

I am certain that slavery still exists not just in its more modern form but also in a form we would expect to exist in the past. We should not be shocked at this because it was not banned a thousand years ago and so its effects will still be with us in some way. The problem here is that it was not you that stood in what was named "The Old Slave Traders Bar" as I was, it was not you that got kidnapped and hypnotized kidnappers, and it was not you that worked out slavery existed there and possibly just narrowly escaped this same fate myself. But slavery exists and so we must be cautious when working this magick; cautious not to tell others if we live in a country we think slavery could exist in at all because it is alive and well and those profiting from it would certainly attack if they thought they would lose out. But do use what follows do that we collectively can attack slavery and help to stop its existence forever. Will this magick to work with your strongest force.

Superhero magick to free slaves and powerless people

Papa Legba the Voodoo Man himself, he known as Saint Peter, the old man with walking cane and with stick in hand you walk with a limp but only because you have one foot always in one world and the other foot in another because you control the doorway that swings many ways and to many places. Papa Legba open the doorway, open the doorway here and now: Papa Legba does open the doorway, the doorway opens it is open here and now. I call Ti-Jean-Petro the one-legged dwarf, the powerful mage through the doorway. Ti-Jean-Petro come through the doorway and be here with me: Ti-Jean-Petro does come through the doorway and is here with me. Ti-Jean-Petro I ask that you free all slaves and powerless people and this is what I ask of you. Ti-Jean-Petro agrees to help and departs back through the doorway. Papa Legba the Voodoo Man himself, he known as Saint Peter, the old man with walking cane and with stick in hand you walk with a limp but only because you have one foot always in one world and the other foot in another because you control the doorway that swings many ways and to many places. Papa Legba shut the doorway, shut the doorway here and now: Papa Legba does shut the doorway, the doorway closes it is shut here and now. So it is and will be.

There are those that enslave others and these people are perhaps of the worst kind: who else is worse than a slave maker. I wish the world to be free of such people and so I offer magick to help this to occur. However, for this magick to work it needs you to say the words which follow while truly intending them to work. If we all do this, we can take a swipe at these evil people and help to make a better world.

Superhero magick to rid the world of enslavers

Papa Legba the Voodoo Man himself, he known as Saint Peter, the old man with walking cane and with stick in hand you walk with a

limp but only because you have one foot always in one world and the other foot in another because you control the doorway that swings many ways and to many places. Papa Legba open the doorway, open the doorway here and now: Papa Legba does open the doorway, the doorway opens it is open here and now. I call Ti-Jean-Petro the one-legged dwarf, the powerful mage through the doorway. Ti-Jean-Petro come through the doorway and be here with me: Ti-Jean-Petro does come through the doorway and is here with me. Ti-Jean-Petro I ask that you attack all enslavers and all slave-makers of all kinds, rid the world of them and this is what I ask of you. Ti-Jean-Petro agrees to help and departs back through the doorway. Papa Legba the Voodoo Man himself, he known as Saint Peter, the old man with walking cane and with stick in hand you walk with a limp but only because you have one foot always in one world and the other foot in another because you control the doorway that swings many ways and to many places. Papa Legba shut the doorway, shut the doorway here and now: Papa Legba does shut the doorway, the doorway closes it is shut here and now. So it is and will be.

There does exist people who have no power: or little. I feel a good thing to do is to empower these people so they will not have to deal with such a terrible life. While it is true that only the slave is truly powerless there are many such slaves as these do work this magick and help them gain power even if they had not it before.

Superhero magick to empower the powerless

Papa Legba the Voodoo Man himself, he known as Saint Peter, the old man with walking cane and with stick in hand you walk with a limp but only because you have one foot always in one world and the other foot in another because you control the doorway that swings many ways and to many places. Papa Legba open the doorway, open the doorway here and now: Papa Legba does open

the doorway, the doorway opens it is open here and now. I call Ti-Jean-Petro the one-legged dwarf, the powerful mage through the doorway. Ti-Jean-Petro come through the doorway and be here with me: Ti-Jean-Petro does come through the doorway and is here with me. Ti-Jean-Petro I ask that you empower the powerless and this is what I ask of you. Ti-Jean-Petro agrees to help and departs back through the doorway. Papa Legba the Voodoo Man himself, he known as Saint Peter, the old man with walking cane and with stick in hand you walk with a limp but only because you have one foot always in one world and the other foot in another because you control the doorway that swings many ways and to many places. Papa Legba shut the doorway, shut the doorway here and now: Papa Legba does shut the doorway, the doorway closes it is shut here and now. So it is and will be.

I know that our collective civilization runs not just on freedom but also on a lack of it as we give away some rights to be safer and to let civilization flourish because civilization isn't about everyone doing as they wish, but is also about what works for the whole of us. However, I think that our rulers have taken away too much of our freedom and so here is magick to give everyone more freedom.

Superhero magick to give everyone more freedom

Papa Legba the Voodoo Man himself, he known as Saint Peter, the old man with walking cane and with stick in hand you walk with a limp but only because you have one foot always in one world and the other foot in another because you control the doorway that swings many ways and to many places. Papa Legba open the doorway, open the doorway here and now: Papa Legba does open the doorway, the doorway opens it is open here and now. I call Ti-Jean-Petro the one-legged dwarf, the powerful mage through the doorway. Ti-Jean-Petro come through the doorway and be here with me: Ti-Jean-Petro does come through the doorway and is here with me. Ti-Jean-Petro I ask that you give more freedom to everyone and this is what I ask of you. Ti-Jean-Petro agrees to help and departs back through the doorway. Papa Legba the Voodoo Man himself, he known as Saint Peter, the old man with walking cane and with stick in hand you walk with a limp but only because you have one foot always in one world and the other foot in another because you control the doorway that swings many ways and to many places. Papa Legba shut the doorway, shut the doorway here and now: Papa Legba does shut the doorway, the doorway closes it is shut here and now. So it is and will be.

You are starting to work magick to affect everyone for the good: something only a true superhero could do. That's right you are now a superhero and this is because of the deeds you have done through this magick: your superpower if you had not guessed is magick itself.

Chapter 3 Healing

To heal is a power and certainly I think anyone with this ability is surely the owner of a legitimate superpower however it was gained and no matter what type of healing they are doing. I wish you to have the power to heal but I also do not want you to think that magick is the only way to heal and I feel we should use personally whatever works. I say this because I am a fan of medicine and yet I still wish to offer this magick that follows to heal everyone at a location of your choosing. However, it is easier to get this magick to work if you are familiar with the location: if not look at it on a map, look at pictures and video if you can. Will what follows to work and it shall.

Superhero magick to heal everyone at a chosen location

Papa Legba the Voodoo Man himself, he known as Saint Peter, the old man with walking cane and with stick in hand you walk with a

limp but only because you have one foot always in one world and the other foot in another because you control the doorway that swings many ways and to many places. Papa Legba open the doorway, open the doorway here and now: Papa Legba does open the doorway, the doorway opens it is open here and now. I call Ti-Jean-Petro the one-legged dwarf, the powerful mage through the doorway. Ti-Jean-Petro come through the doorway and be here with me: Ti-Jean-Petro does come through the doorway and is here with me. Ti-Jean-Petro I ask that you heal everyone at, within and around state address or chosen location so they will be illness and problem free and this is what I ask of you. Ti-Jean-Petro agrees to help and departs back through the doorway. Papa Legba the Voodoo Man himself, he known as Saint Peter, the old man with walking cane and with stick in hand you walk with a limp but only because you have one foot always in one world and the other foot in another because you control the doorway that swings many ways and to many places. Papa Legba shut the doorway, shut the doorway here and now: Papa Legba does shut the doorway, the doorway closes it is shut here and now. So it is and will be.

One good person to be able to heal is yourself. I know this may sound a selfish thing but it is difficult to help others if we ourselves are not in good condition. I feel that saving yourself is no less laudable than saving another. Also, it is true that the superhero way seems to be very much about looking after ourselves or at least being as well as we can: the supervillain way is quite different to this regard and I have written many supervillain magick books: to find them type S Rob supervillains or supervillains in a search engine. Will this magick to be healed and you will find it will help you.

Superhero magick to heal yourself

Papa Legba the Voodoo Man himself, he known as Saint Peter, the old man with walking cane and with stick in hand you walk with a limp but only because you have one foot always in one world and the other foot in another because you control the doorway that swings many ways and to many places. Papa Legba open the doorway, open the doorway here and now: Papa Legba does open the doorway, the doorway opens it is open here and now. I call Ti-Jean-Petro the one-legged dwarf, the powerful mage through the doorway. Ti-Jean-Petro come through the doorway and be here with me: Ti-Jean-Petro does come through the doorway and is here with me. Ti-Jean-Petro I ask that you heal me heal me of all illnesses and problems, heal me of weaknesses and this is what I ask of you. Ti-Jean-Petro agrees to help and departs back through the doorway. Papa Legba the Voodoo Man himself, he known as Saint Peter, the old man with walking cane and with stick in hand you walk with a limp but only because you have one foot always in one world and the other foot in another because you control the doorway that swings many ways and to many places. Papa Legba shut the doorway, shut the doorway here and now: Papa Legba does shut the doorway, the doorway closes it is shut here and now. So it is and will be.

This following magick is to heal anyone of your choosing: it works best on someone who you know well enough to know their name and what they look like. I would like to add however that these details can be found out through research. This magick follows now.

Superhero magick to heal a chosen person

Papa Legba the Voodoo Man himself, he known as Saint Peter, the old man with walking cane and with stick in hand you walk with a limp but only because you have one foot always in one world and the other foot in another because you control the doorway that swings many ways and to many places. Papa Legba open the doorway, open the doorway here and now: Papa Legba does open the doorway, the doorway opens it is open here and now. I call Ti-Jean-Petro the one-legged dwarf, the powerful mage through the doorway. Ti-Jean-Petro come through the doorway and be here with me: Ti-Jean-Petro does come through the doorway and is here with me. Ti-Jean-Petro I ask that you heal <u>state name of chosen person</u> heal them of all illness and weakness heal them of all problems and this is what I ask of you. Ti-Jean-Petro agrees to help and departs back through the doorway. Papa Legba the Voodoo Man himself, he known as Saint Peter, the old man with walking cane and with stick in hand you walk with a limp but only because you have one foot always in one world and the other foot in another because you control the doorway that swings many ways and to many places. Papa Legba shut the doorway, shut the doorway here

24

and now: Papa Legba does shut the doorway, the doorway closes it is shut here and now. So it is and will be.

If we have family still alive, we will want to help them through healing. I understand that in reality we shall need to heal our family because what happens to them often happens to us too. I feel that in life we need to do this so that we can help others without fear.

Superhero magick to heal your family

Papa Legba the Voodoo Man himself, he known as Saint Peter, the old man with walking cane and with stick in hand you walk with a limp but only because you have one foot always in one world and the other foot in another because you control the doorway that swings many ways and to many places. Papa Legba open the doorway, open the doorway here and now: Papa Legba does open the doorway, the doorway opens it is open here and now. I call Ti-Jean-Petro the one-legged dwarf, the powerful mage through the

doorway. Ti-Jean-Petro come through the doorway and be here with me: Ti-Jean-Petro does come through the doorway and is here with me. Ti-Jean-Petro I ask that you heal my family, heal them of all illness and problems and this is what I ask of you. Ti-Jean-Petro agrees to help and departs back through the doorway. Papa Legba the Voodoo Man himself, he known as Saint Peter, the old man with walking cane and with stick in hand you walk with a limp but only because you have one foot always in one world and the other foot in another because you control the doorway that swings many ways and to many places. Papa Legba shut the doorway, shut the doorway here and now: Papa Legba does shut the doorway, the doorway closes it is shut here and now. So it is and will be.

You have expanded the range of magick you can do and also expanded the range of magick you understand meaning that this apparent weirdness in the world is now understood to be simply a part of how things work. You have stretched yourself and have

26

become more than you were: you are becoming a magical

superhero.

Chapter 4 Law and morality

The superhero is never really above the law they may appear to be outside of it but in reality, wishes the law and order system as much strength as it can have. This following magick is simply to help law and order to remain in place: this magick follows, here it is.

Superhero magick for law and order to remain in place in a chosen location

Papa Legba the Voodoo Man himself, he known as Saint Peter, the old man with walking cane and with stick in hand you walk with a limp but only because you have one foot always in one world and the other foot in another because you control the doorway that swings many ways and to many places. Papa Legba open the doorway, open the doorway here and now: Papa Legba does open the doorway, the doorway opens it is open here and now. I call Ti-Jean-Petro the one-legged dwarf, the powerful mage through the

doorway. Ti-Jean-Petro come through the doorway and be here with me: Ti-Jean-Petro does come through the doorway and is here with me. Ti-Jean-Petro I ask that you make it so that law and order rule in state chosen address or location and this is what I ask of you. Ti-Jean-Petro agrees to help and departs back through the doorway. Papa Legba the Voodoo Man himself, he known as Saint Peter, the old man with walking cane and with stick in hand you walk with a limp but only because you have one foot always in one world and the other foot in another because you control the doorway that swings many ways and to many places. Papa Legba shut the doorway, shut the doorway here and now: Papa Legba does shut the doorway, the doorway closes it is shut here and now. So it is and will be.

It is hard to live without justice and while it is true that we need to understand this we also can help another have justice. Many people have had bad life events and these often are not of the type where we ever gain justice. I want everyone to have justice and so I let you choose who you wish to help hoping you decide to help many more.

Superhero magick for justice for a chosen person

Papa Legba the Voodoo Man himself, he known as Saint Peter, the old man with walking cane and with stick in hand you walk with a limp but only because you have one foot always in one world and the other foot in another because you control the doorway that swings many ways and to many places. Papa Legba open the doorway, open the doorway here and now: Papa Legba does open the doorway, the doorway opens it is open here and now. I call Ti-Jean-Petro the one-legged dwarf, the powerful mage through the doorway. Ti-Jean-Petro come through the doorway and be here with me: Ti-Jean-Petro does come through the doorway and is here with me. Ti-Jean-Petro I ask that you make it so that justice will assist <u>state name of chosen person</u> so that injustices in their life will

30

be transformed into justice and law and order and fairness and this is what I ask of you. Ti-Jean-Petro agrees to help and departs back through the doorway. Papa Legba the Voodoo Man himself, he known as Saint Peter, the old man with walking cane and with stick in hand you walk with a limp but only because you have one foot always in one world and the other foot in another because you control the doorway that swings many ways and to many places. Papa Legba shut the doorway, shut the doorway here and now: Papa Legba does shut the doorway, the doorway closes it is shut here and now. So it is and will be.

This magick changes how people think and yet the superhero is largely an example as much as anything. The point of superheroes for many isn't the actual events they are in but the example they set for the rest of the world. However, this magick can help a set of people all in the same location to act morally.

Superhero magick for morality to rule in a chosen location

Papa Legba the Voodoo Man himself, he known as Saint Peter, the old man with walking cane and with stick in hand you walk with a limp but only because you have one foot always in one world and the other foot in another because you control the doorway that swings many ways and to many places. Papa Legba open the doorway, open the doorway here and now: Papa Legba does open the doorway, the doorway opens it is open here and now. I call Ti-Jean-Petro the one-legged dwarf, the powerful mage through the doorway. Ti-Jean-Petro come through the doorway and be here with me: Ti-Jean-Petro does come through the doorway and is here with me. Ti-Jean-Petro I ask that you make it so that morality rules in <u>state chosen address or location</u> and this is what I ask of you. Ti-Jean-Petro agrees to help and departs back through the doorway. Papa Legba the Voodoo Man himself, he known as Saint Peter, the old man with walking cane and with stick in hand you walk with a limp but only because you have one foot always in one world and the other foot in another because you control the doorway that swings many ways and to many places. Papa Legba shut the doorway, shut the doorway here and now: Papa Legba does shut the doorway, the doorway closes it is shut here and now. So it is and will be.

There are times when in life the outcome relies upon the actions of some small set of people, perhaps one man even. I feel this following magick is perfect for these situations when you or even the world needs a specific person to act justly. If you wish what follows to work you will discover that it does.

Superhero magick for a chosen person to act justly

Papa Legba the Voodoo Man himself, he known as Saint Peter, the old man with walking cane and with stick in hand you walk with a limp but only because you have one foot always in one world and the other foot in another because you control the doorway that swings many ways and to many places. Papa Legba open the doorway, open the doorway here and now: Papa Legba does open the doorway, the doorway opens it is open here and now. I call Ti-Jean-Petro the one-legged dwarf, the powerful mage through the doorway. Ti-Jean-Petro come through the doorway and be here with me: Ti-Jean-Petro does come through the doorway and is here with me. Ti-Jean-Petro I ask that you make it so that state name of chosen person will act justly and this is what I ask of you. Ti-Jean-Petro agrees to help and departs back through the doorway. Papa Legba the Voodoo Man himself, he known as Saint Peter, the old man with walking cane and with stick in hand you walk with a limp but only because you have one foot always in one world and the other foot in another because you control the doorway that swings many ways and to many places. Papa Legba shut the doorway, shut the doorway here and now: Papa Legba does shut the doorway, the doorway closes it is shut here and now. So it is and will be.

It may be of interest to you that when writing this the world is in the throes of the Coronavirus outbreak already labelled a pandemic and yet as yet: the 18th of march 2020: there are diseases that have killed many, many, more people. But don't think that this magick is for times that are far away because right now people need magick and they need to be able to remain calm and often the world of occultism can give a strength and differing view of the world that is beneficial. But this is a great example of how superheroes exist because medicine is a subject that is based on helping people, it is the art and science of the healer. This magick in this chapter however is about law and order and morality and if these break down they will not be because of the virus they will be because of the way people have acted and so I feel the best way to help civilization to remain and to reduce negative social effects is to use this magick and to uphold the rule of law and order. The structure of the world can remain solid I simply ask that you think on this perhaps from times in a far-off future and know that when needed occultists were there.

Chapter 5 Revenge and avenging

Any one of us can get items stolen. We are the ones therefore that we must help and so I offer this magick to assist you. I am aware however that not everyone gets things stolen and that some people have not had anything stolen that they can recall but perhaps it is simply that they cannot remember the item being stolen because of its trivial nature or that they thought they lost the item when it was stolen all along. I therefore present this next magick.

Superhero magick to get a stolen item back

Papa Legba the Voodoo Man himself, he known as Saint Peter, the old man with walking cane and with stick in hand you walk with a limp but only because you have one foot always in one world and the other foot in another because you control the doorway that swings many ways and to many places. Papa Legba open the doorway, open the doorway here and now: Papa Legba does open

the doorway, the doorway opens it is open here and now. I call Ti-Jean-Petro the one-legged dwarf, the powerful mage through the doorway. Ti-Jean-Petro come through the doorway and be here with me: Ti-Jean-Petro does come through the doorway and is here with me. Ti-Jean-Petro I ask that you make it so that I shall get name stolen item back, so that it will be mine again and this is what I ask of you. Ti-Jean-Petro agrees to help and departs back through the doorway. Papa Legba the Voodoo Man himself, he known as Saint Peter, the old man with walking cane and with stick in hand you walk with a limp but only because you have one foot always in one world and the other foot in another because you control the doorway that swings many ways and to many places. Papa Legba shut the doorway, shut the doorway here and now: Papa Legba does shut the doorway, the doorway closes it is shut here and now. So it is and will be.

It is quite possible that you could get attacked and for a superhero this is considered to be part of the job. I however think that magick should help out any occult superhero and so here is magick that will help you. If you intend and will this magick to work you will see that it does.

Superhero magick for all attackers to get attacked

Papa Legba the Voodoo Man himself, he known as Saint Peter, the old man with walking cane and with stick in hand you walk with a limp but only because you have one foot always in one world and the other foot in another because you control the doorway that swings many ways and to many places. Papa Legba open the doorway, open the doorway here and now: Papa Legba does open the doorway, the doorway opens it is open here and now. I call Ti-Jean-Petro the one-legged dwarf, the powerful mage through the doorway. Ti-Jean-Petro come through the doorway and be here with me: Ti-Jean-Petro does come through the doorway and is here with me. Ti-Jean-Petro I ask that you make it so that all who have attacked me shall get attacked and this is what I ask of you. Ti-Jean-Petro agrees to help and departs back through the doorway. Papa Legba the Voodoo Man himself, he known as Saint Peter, the old man with walking cane and with stick in hand you walk with a limp but only because you have one foot always in one world and the other foot in another because you control the doorway that swings many ways and to many places. Papa Legba shut the doorway, shut the doorway here and now: Papa Legba does shut the doorway, the doorway closes it is shut here and now. So it is and will be.

There are times when what is deserved isn't justice but revenge: for someone to be avenged for some terrible deed. I understand that the world frequently surprises us because we live in such interesting times. To avenge a person of your choosing simply use this following magick.

Superhero magick to avenge a chosen person

Papa Legba the Voodoo Man himself, he known as Saint Peter, the old man with walking cane and with stick in hand you walk with a limp but only because you have one foot always in one world and the other foot in another because you control the doorway that swings many ways and to many places. Papa Legba open the doorway, open the doorway here and now: Papa Legba does open the doorway, the doorway opens it is open here and now. I call Ti-Jean-Petro the one-legged dwarf, the powerful mage through the doorway. Ti-Jean-Petro come through the doorway and be here with me: Ti-Jean-Petro does come through the doorway and is here with me. Ti-Jean-Petro I ask that you avenge state name of chosen person so that all unfairness and attacks that have happened to them are avenged, and this is what I ask of you. Ti-Jean-Petro agrees to help and departs back through the doorway. Papa Legba the Voodoo Man himself, he known as Saint Peter, the old man with

41

walking cane and with stick in hand you walk with a limp but only because you have one foot always in one world and the other foot in another because you control the doorway that swings many ways and to many places. Papa Legba shut the doorway, shut the doorway here and now: Papa Legba does shut the doorway, the doorway closes it is shut here and now. So it is and will be.

Dictators are to me the evilest of all people because they do evil on mass, they kill, torture and cheat on a large scale: much larger than they ever could if they were not a dictator. I feel the world would function better without any dictators. But together we have the power to remove them: or at least make their lives more difficult and their reins less pleasurable and this magick follows now.

Superhero magick to destroy all dictators

Papa Legba the Voodoo Man himself, he known as Saint Peter, the old man with walking cane and with stick in hand you walk with a

limp but only because you have one foot always in one world and the other foot in another because you control the doorway that swings many ways and to many places. Papa Legba open the doorway, open the doorway here and now: Papa Legba does open the doorway, the doorway opens it is open here and now. I call Ti-Jean-Petro the one-legged dwarf, the powerful mage through the doorway. Ti-Jean-Petro come through the doorway and be here with me: Ti-Jean-Petro does come through the doorway and is here with me. Ti-Jean-Petro I ask that you destroy all dictators so that they shall not rule anymore and this is what I ask of you. Ti-Jean-Petro agrees to help and departs back through the doorway. Papa Legba the Voodoo Man himself, he known as Saint Peter, the old man with walking cane and with stick in hand you walk with a limp but only because you have one foot always in one world and the other foot in another because you control the doorway that swings many ways and to many places. Papa Legba shut the doorway, shut the doorway here and now: Papa Legba does shut the doorway, the doorway closes it is shut here and now. So it is and will be.

People do lie and this means that people lie to us and this can present many problems. I understand this and so offer magick to help you. In fact, this next magick is so you will know when you are being lied to: will what follows to work and it shall.

Superhero magick to know when people lie to you

Papa Legba the Voodoo Man himself, he known as Saint Peter, the old man with walking cane and with stick in hand you walk with a limp but only because you have one foot always in one world and the other foot in another because you control the doorway that swings many ways and to many places. Papa Legba open the doorway, open the doorway here and now: Papa Legba does open the doorway, the doorway opens it is open here and now. I call Ti-Jean-Petro the one-legged dwarf, the powerful mage through the

doorway. Ti-Jean-Petro come through the doorway and be here with me: Ti-Jean-Petro does come through the doorway and is here with me. Ti-Jean-Petro I ask that you make it so that I know when people lie to me and this is what I ask of you. Ti-Jean-Petro agrees to help and departs back through the doorway. Papa Legba the Voodoo Man himself, he known as Saint Peter, the old man with walking cane and with stick in hand you walk with a limp but only because you have one foot always in one world and the other foot in another because you control the doorway that swings many ways and to many places. Papa Legba shut the doorway, shut the doorway here and now: Papa Legba does shut the doorway, the doorway closes it is shut here and now. So it is and will be.

As you have read through these pages and gotten to this point you have gained in experience and wisdom because only the wise know that everything is not known to them and experience in magick is gained in the doing and this is easily gotten through saying the words that are here. Be proud of your achievements but remember that as you work your way through the book that there is more to come.

Chapter 6 Thwarting supervillains

The superhero must eventually find at least one good supervillain and yet doing so makes life more difficult. I suppose this is no less the truth because you will need to know where they reside and so possibly know their secret hideout and this is what this next magick is for and so after working it do keep your eyes out for signs pointing the way that a supervillains may reside.

Superhero magick to know where the nearest supervillain resides

Papa Legba the Voodoo Man himself, he known as Saint Peter, the old man with walking cane and with stick in hand you walk with a limp but only because you have one foot always in one world and the other foot in another because you control the doorway that swings many ways and to many places. Papa Legba open the doorway, open the doorway here and now: Papa Legba does open

the doorway, the doorway opens it is open here and now. I call Ti-Jean-Petro the one-legged dwarf, the powerful mage through the doorway. Ti-Jean-Petro come through the doorway and be here with me: Ti-Jean-Petro does come through the doorway and is here with me. Ti-Jean-Petro I ask that you make it so that I know where the nearest supervillain resides and this is what I ask of you. Ti-Jean-Petro agrees to help and departs back through the doorway. Papa Legba the Voodoo Man himself, he known as Saint Peter, the old man with walking cane and with stick in hand you walk with a limp but only because you have one foot always in one world and the other foot in another because you control the doorway that swings many ways and to many places. Papa Legba shut the doorway, shut the doorway here and now: Papa Legba does shut the doorway, the doorway closes it is shut here and now. So it is and will be.

Supervillains have plans in fact making plans is the mark of any supervillains: this magick however will work on any villains helping you to thwart the plans they have. Think of this magick as a magical assistant helping you to achieve this goal. Yes, there will be something you are likely to need to do to thwart the plans and you must decide what it is but this magick that follows will help.

Superhero magick to be able to thwart villains' plans

Papa Legba the Voodoo Man himself, he known as Saint Peter, the old man with walking cane and with stick in hand you walk with a limp but only because you have one foot always in one world and the other foot in another because you control the doorway that swings many ways and to many places. Papa Legba open the doorway, open the doorway here and now: Papa Legba does open the doorway, the doorway opens it is open here and now. I call Ti-Jean-Petro the one-legged dwarf, the powerful mage through the doorway. Ti-Jean-Petro come through the doorway and be here with me: Ti-Jean-Petro does come through the doorway and is here with me. Ti-Jean-Petro I ask that you make it so that I will be able to thwart villains plans and this is what I ask of you. Ti-Jean-Petro agrees to help and departs back through the doorway. Papa Legba the Voodoo Man himself, he known as Saint Peter, the old man with walking cane and with stick in hand you walk with a limp but only because you have one foot always in one world and the other foot in another because you control the doorway that swings many ways and to many places. Papa Legba shut the doorway, shut the doorway here and now: Papa Legba does shut the doorway, the doorway closes it is shut here and now. So it is and will be.

Villains often have some form of power and may be powerful people in their own right. However, this means that a villain disempowered is a lot less dangerous and substantially less of a threat and may be easily dealt with by you or others. Will what follows to work and it shall.

Superhero magick to disempower a villain

Papa Legba the Voodoo Man himself, he known as Saint Peter, the old man with walking cane and with stick in hand you walk with a limp but only because you have one foot always in one world and the other foot in another because you control the doorway that swings many ways and to many places. Papa Legba open the doorway, open the doorway here and now: Papa Legba does open the doorway, the doorway opens it is open here and now. I call Ti-Jean-Petro the one-legged dwarf, the powerful mage through the doorway. Ti-Jean-Petro come through the doorway and be here with me: Ti-Jean-Petro does come through the doorway and is here with me. Ti-Jean-Petro I ask that you help me to disempower a villain and this is what I ask of you. Ti-Jean-Petro agrees to help and departs back through the doorway. Papa Legba the Voodoo Man himself, he known as Saint Peter, the old man with walking cane and with stick in hand you walk with a limp but only because you have one foot always in one world and the other foot in another because you control the doorway that swings many ways and to many places. Papa Legba shut the doorway, shut the doorway here and now: Papa Legba does shut the doorway, the doorway closes it is shut here and now. So it is and will be.

Making progress as a superhero is often about keeping going because in the life of an occult superhero staying around counts for a lot. In fact, you would need to be there even in difficult times. You need to fight evil in all its forms and of course be a symbol for what is right so that most of your positive impact is as an inspiration for others. This is right helping people is not the main part of the job but being seen or known to help others to inspire others. However, to inspire others you must also embody strength, if you can intellect and goodness: a high target I agree.

Superhero magick to undermine villains' plans

Papa Legba the Voodoo Man himself, he known as Saint Peter, the old man with walking cane and with stick in hand you walk with a limp but only because you have one foot always in one world and the other foot in another because you control the doorway that swings many ways and to many places. Papa Legba open the doorway, open the doorway here and now: Papa Legba does open the doorway, the doorway opens it is open here and now. I call Ti-Jean-Petro the one-legged dwarf, the powerful mage through the doorway. Ti-Jean-Petro come through the doorway and be here with me: Ti-Jean-Petro does come through the doorway and is here with me. Ti-Jean-Petro I ask that you help me undermine villains plans and this is what I ask of you. Ti-Jean-Petro agrees to help and departs back through the doorway. Papa Legba the Voodoo Man himself, he known as Saint Peter, the old man with walking cane and with stick in hand you walk with a limp but only because you have one foot always in one world and the other foot in another because you control the doorway that swings many ways and to many places. Papa Legba shut the doorway, shut the doorway here and now: Papa Legba does shut the doorway, the doorway closes it is shut here and now. So it is and will be.

The truth is that you now have a good idea of the meat and potatoes end of being an occult superhero. However, you will need to learn more so do continue to work through the book and apart from this you don't even need to wear your underpants outside of your trousers. That right I think the best place for underwear for any occult supervillain is below out outside clothes.

Chapter 7 Wealth

Wealth is a factor in almost everyone's life: everyone who isn't a monk, or nun. This means that having wealth will actually increase how many people you can help or perhaps make the helping of others easier on you: less of a stress. I therefore, now show magick for great wealth; here it is.

Superhero magick for great wealth

Papa Legba the Voodoo Man himself, he known as Saint Peter, the old man with walking cane and with stick in hand you walk with a limp but only because you have one foot always in one world and the other foot in another because you control the doorway that swings many ways and to many places. Papa Legba open the doorway, open the doorway here and now: Papa Legba does open the doorway, the doorway opens it is open here and now. I call Ti-Jean-Petro the one-legged dwarf, the powerful mage through the

doorway. Ti-Jean-Petro come through the doorway and be here with me: Ti-Jean-Petro does come through the doorway and is here with me. Ti-Jean-Petro I ask that you make me greatly rich, make great wealth mine and this is what I ask of you. Ti-Jean-Petro agrees to help and departs back through the doorway. Papa Legba the Voodoo Man himself, he known as Saint Peter, the old man with walking cane and with stick in hand you walk with a limp but only because you have one foot always in one world and the other foot in another because you control the doorway that swings many ways and to many places. Papa Legba shut the doorway, shut the doorway here and now: Papa Legba does shut the doorway, the doorway closes it is shut here and now. So it is and will be.

This next magick is for you to have the power to make a chosen organization rich. To do this all you need do is to say these words with a strong will and real magick will be done. But choose the organization carefully because some organizations will do evil things when they get more resources you must choose an organization that will only do good for society.

Superhero magick to make a chosen organization rich

Papa Legba the Voodoo Man himself, he known as Saint Peter, the old man with walking cane and with stick in hand you walk with a limp but only because you have one foot always in one world and the other foot in another because you control the doorway that swings many ways and to many places. Papa Legba open the doorway, open the doorway here and now: Papa Legba does open the doorway, the doorway opens it is open here and now. I call Ti-Jean-Petro the one-legged dwarf, the powerful mage through the doorway. Ti-Jean-Petro come through the doorway and be here with me: Ti-Jean-Petro does come through the doorway and is here with me. Ti-Jean-Petro I ask that you make state name of chosen organization rich, make great wealth theirs and this is what I ask of you. Ti-Jean-Petro agrees to help and departs back through the doorway. Papa Legba the Voodoo Man himself, he known as Saint Peter, the old man with walking cane and with stick in hand you walk with a limp but only because you have one foot always in one world and the other foot in another because you control the doorway that swings many ways and to many places. Papa Legba shut the doorway, shut the doorway here and now: Papa Legba does shut the doorway, the doorway closes it is shut here and now. So it is and will be.

If you are a real estate investor mortgages are simply a financial strategy whereas for many people a mortgage is simply debt placed on where they live. This all means that a real estate investor may want mortgages and not wish to pay them off at all: keep them perpetually: however, the normal house dweller finds that the time their mortgage is paid off a great time because it removes one cost from their lives. This means you should be careful who you are trying to help with this magick: pick people you know well.

Superhero magick to enable a chosen person to be mortgage free

Papa Legba the Voodoo Man himself, he known as Saint Peter, the old man with walking cane and with stick in hand you walk with a limp but only because you have one foot always in one world and the other foot in another because you control the doorway that swings many ways and to many places. Papa Legba open the doorway, open the doorway here and now: Papa Legba does open the doorway, the doorway opens it is open here and now. I call Ti-Jean-Petro the one-legged dwarf, the powerful mage through the doorway. Ti-Jean-Petro come through the doorway and be here with me: Ti-Jean-Petro does come through the doorway and is here with me. Ti-Jean-Petro I ask that you help state name of chosen person become mortgage free and this is what I ask of you. Ti-Jean-Petro agrees to help and departs back through the doorway. Papa Legba the Voodoo Man himself, he known as Saint Peter, the old man with walking cane and with stick in hand you walk with a limp but only because you have one foot always in one world and the other foot in another because you control the doorway that swings many ways and to many places. Papa Legba shut the doorway, shut the doorway here and now: Papa Legba does shut the doorway, the doorway closes it is shut here and now. So it is and will be.

Getting a proper superhero lair is difficult and so I have here some magick to help you. I know that a superhero lair is something difficult to find because such real estate is always of interest to superheroes and supervillains and so don't be surprised if you most well-known supervillain rival wants the same place as you. But this magick will help and here it is.

Superhero magick for a superhero lair

Papa Legba the Voodoo Man himself, he known as Saint Peter, the old man with walking cane and with stick in hand you walk with a limp but only because you have one foot always in one world and the other foot in another because you control the doorway that swings many ways and to many places. Papa Legba open the doorway, open the doorway here and now: Papa Legba does open the doorway, the doorway opens it is open here and now. I call Ti-Jean-Petro the one-legged dwarf, the powerful mage through the doorway. Ti-Jean-Petro come through the doorway and be here with me: Ti-Jean-Petro does come through the doorway and is here with me. Ti-Jean-Petro I ask that you help me gain a superhero lair and this is what I ask of you. Ti-Jean-Petro agrees to help and departs back through the doorway. Papa Legba the Voodoo Man himself, he known as Saint Peter, the old man with walking cane and with stick in hand you walk with a limp but only because you have one foot always in one world and the other foot in another because you control the doorway that swings many ways and to many places. Papa Legba shut the doorway, shut the doorway here and now: Papa Legba does shut the doorway, the doorway closes it is shut here and now. So it is and will be.

Everything is easier with some money even being a superhero and this is why this next magick exists. I feel that a superhero should have some money flowing to them simply because they will find everything is better both their personal life and their superhero existence. I feel you should choose to work this following magick.

Superhero magick for money to flow to you

Papa Legba the Voodoo Man himself, he known as Saint Peter, the old man with walking cane and with stick in hand you walk with a limp but only because you have one foot always in one world and the other foot in another because you control the doorway that swings many ways and to many places. Papa Legba open the doorway, open the doorway here and now: Papa Legba does open the doorway, the doorway opens it is open here and now. I call Ti-Jean-Petro the one-legged dwarf, the powerful mage through the doorway. Ti-Jean-Petro come through the doorway and be here with me: Ti-Jean-Petro does come through the doorway and is here with me. Ti-Jean-Petro I ask that you make money flow to me always and this is what I ask of you. Ti-Jean-Petro agrees to help and departs back through the doorway. Papa Legba the Voodoo Man himself, he known as Saint Peter, the old man with walking cane and with stick in hand you walk with a limp but only because you have one foot always in one world and the other foot in another because you control the doorway that swings many ways and to many places. Papa Legba shut the doorway, shut the doorway here and now: Papa Legba does shut the doorway, the doorway closes it is shut here and now. So it is and will be.

Learn your lessons my dear student because soon your will discovers that for those chosen or that choose themselves to take on the task of superherodom that challenges are a part of the path. At each and every turn you must learn and gain experience because the superhero must have some way of testing himself or herself because it is a changing path, the target keeps moving position but it is so rewarding you will wonder how you managed to live without it.

Chapter 8 Fame and media

It is easier being a superhero if you have some degree of fame. The truth is that fame means you can help good causes without having to do much at all. Indeed, this is why this next magick is more important to you than other people because a superhero can do good works through fame whereas others simply look to be glorified. Will what follows to work strongly and it shall work strongly.

Superhero magick to be famous

Papa Legba the Voodoo Man himself, he known as Saint Peter, the old man with walking cane and with stick in hand you walk with a limp but only because you have one foot always in one world and the other foot in another because you control the doorway that swings many ways and to many places. Papa Legba open the doorway, open the doorway here and now: Papa Legba does open

the doorway, the doorway opens it is open here and now. I call Ti-Jean-Petro the one-legged dwarf, the powerful mage through the doorway. Ti-Jean-Petro come through the doorway and be here with me: Ti-Jean-Petro does come through the doorway and is here with me. Ti-Jean-Petro I ask that you help me become famous and this is what I ask of you. Ti-Jean-Petro agrees to help and departs back through the doorway. Papa Legba the Voodoo Man himself, he known as Saint Peter, the old man with walking cane and with stick in hand you walk with a limp but only because you have one foot always in one world and the other foot in another because you control the doorway that swings many ways and to many places. Papa Legba shut the doorway, shut the doorway here and now: Papa Legba does shut the doorway, the doorway closes it is shut here and now. So it is and will be.

Because you are a superhero you do indeed help others and so here follows some magick to make another person famous. This magick may want you to consider if the person is really suited to fame or whether they do not seem to be at all.

Superhero magick to make a chosen person famous

Papa Legba the Voodoo Man himself, he known as Saint Peter, the old man with walking cane and with stick in hand you walk with a limp but only because you have one foot always in one world and the other foot in another because you control the doorway that swings many ways and to many places. Papa Legba open the doorway, open the doorway here and now: Papa Legba does open the doorway, the doorway opens it is open here and now. I call Ti-Jean-Petro the one-legged dwarf, the powerful mage through the doorway. Ti-Jean-Petro come through the doorway and be here with me: Ti-Jean-Petro does come through the doorway and is here with me. Ti-Jean-Petro I ask that you make state name of chosen person famous and this is what I ask of you. Ti-Jean-Petro agrees to help and departs back through the doorway. Papa Legba the

Voodoo Man himself, he known as Saint Peter, the old man with walking cane and with stick in hand you walk with a limp but only because you have one foot always in one world and the other foot in another because you control the doorway that swings many ways and to many places. Papa Legba shut the doorway, shut the doorway here and now: Papa Legba does shut the doorway, the doorway closes it is shut here and now. So it is and will be.

There are times when serious problems must be tackled and the only way to deal with them is to get attention for them. At the moment I am a member of one of Amnesty Internationals local groups and the truth is there are endless people that need releasing because they have been treat badly, because they have pointed out some human rights violation usually imprisoned and tortured. But there are many other issues and so do use this following magick to make problems of your choice well known.

Superhero magick to make a chosen problem well known

Papa Legba the Voodoo Man himself, he known as Saint Peter, the old man with walking cane and with stick in hand you walk with a limp but only because you have one foot always in one world and the other foot in another because you control the doorway that swings many ways and to many places. Papa Legba open the doorway, open the doorway here and now: Papa Legba does open the doorway, the doorway opens it is open here and now. I call Ti-Jean-Petro the one-legged dwarf, the powerful mage through the doorway. Ti-Jean-Petro come through the doorway and be here with me: Ti-Jean-Petro does come through the doorway and is here with me. Ti-Jean-Petro I ask that you make the problem state problem known to all and this is what I ask of you. Ti-Jean-Petro agrees to help and departs back through the doorway. Papa Legba the Voodoo Man himself, he known as Saint Peter, the old man with walking cane and with stick in hand you walk with a limp but only because you have one foot always in one world and the other foot in another because you control the doorway that swings many ways and to many places. Papa Legba shut the doorway, shut the doorway here and now: Papa Legba does shut the doorway, the doorway closes it is shut here and now. So it is and will be.

The world has many victims of torture and this is the way of the world and yet I personally find it unacceptable. What I am saying is that magick can help and so you will be learning it here. But the truth is that under the dictionary definition I myself suffered torture of a type named pharmacological torture. This is a method whereby someone is given: without choice: a hallucinogenic substance within an interrogation, and in my case, this happened not in my own country but another. In fact, it was done by a branch of their police. I in fact did nothing wrong but I did escape from being kidnapped in the same country using hypnosis and this means that the dishonest local police would not have gotten any money which

70

they otherwise would have gotten. I know why this whole thing happened and one of them you may be holding in your hands right now or at least reading. I was chosen as a target because of the books and the massive number of them I have written which is at the moment approaching 500 and is currently more than anyone else has in history. Occultism is real magick and it offends people and so this was the reason and so along with my world record as easily the most prolific occult author in history I also am a target. I write on because I accepted that this could be my fate long ago. Torture is real.

Superhero magick to free torture victims

Papa Legba the Voodoo Man himself, he known as Saint Peter, the old man with walking cane and with stick in hand you walk with a limp but only because you have one foot always in one world and the other foot in another because you control the doorway that swings many ways and to many places. Papa Legba open the doorway, open the doorway here and now: Papa Legba does open the doorway, the doorway opens it is open here and now. I call Ti-Jean-Petro the one-legged dwarf, the powerful mage through the doorway. Ti-Jean-Petro come through the doorway and be here with me: Ti-Jean-Petro does come through the doorway and is here with me. Ti-Jean-Petro I ask that you help free current victims of torture so they may be free and safe in the world and this is what I ask of you. Ti-Jean-Petro agrees to help and departs back through the doorway. Papa Legba the Voodoo Man himself, he known as Saint Peter, the old man with walking cane and with stick in hand you walk with a limp but only because you have one foot always in one world and the other foot in another because you control the doorway that swings many ways and to many places. Papa Legba shut the doorway, shut the doorway here and now: Papa Legba does shut the doorway, the doorway closes it is shut here and now. So it is and will be.

Magick is real of this you now know and have probably felt some

of its power yourself. However, the fact that magick is a utility

item, it is something that you can use many different ways and to

help others or yourself. If you practice this you are already a

superhero.